OXFAM 50
Our World in Photographs

OXFAM 50

Our World in Photographs

COLLINS & BROWN

First published in Great Britain in 1992
by Collins & Brown Limited
Mercury House
195 Knightsbridge
London SW7 1RE

British Library Cataloguing-in-Publication Data.
A catalogue record for this book
is available from the British Library.

ISBN 1 85585 113 X

Designed and typeset by Toucan Books Limited, London

Reproduction by J. Film, Singapore
Printed and Bound in Hong Kong

Front cover: *Women from Mewell village in Senegal.*

Back cover: *Women going fishing near Kumi, Uganda. As fishing nets, lines and hooks are in short supply, some people still use baskets.*

Title Page: *In many poor families, children work alongside their parents to ensure that the family has enough money to buy food.*

Right: *The day begins in Batenkhali, Bangladesh.*

Contents

Preface

A tidal wave leaves thousands dead in Bangladesh; a typhoon wreaks havoc in Vietnam; a devastating famine hits Ethiopia and Sudan; deep snowfalls threaten the Kurds in northern Iraq. Disasters like these always hit the headlines. The world reels in horror. Aid agencies and the international community mount relief operations. The general public responds with compassion and generosity. Given this catalogue of tragedy, we could be forgiven for thinking that the 'Third World' lurches from crisis to crisis, and that people in developing countries spend most of their lives staving off disasters – floods, droughts, cyclones or wars.

Glossy holiday and travel brochures, on the other hand, invite us to soothe our troubles away on palm-fringed beaches; lose ourselves among the temples of the East; discover adventure and the back-to-nature lifestyle on safari in Africa; or to take up the challenge of a trek in the Himalayas or the Andes. Whether we seek tranquillity or excitement, these popular tourist destinations allow us to experience an idyllic way of life away from the hubbub of the industrialized world.

Disasters and paradise. These conflicting images have tended to dominate our perception of the Third World. Rarely are we provided with an insight into the lives of ordinary people. *Oxfam 50: Our World in Photographs* seeks to fill this gap and to present life as it is actually lived in the developing world.

We see people in their homes, their work places, at the local market, in their villages, towns or cities. A man gets up at dawn to go to work. A woman prepares the first meal of the day. A child sets off to school. We see people growing and preparing food; learning new skills; working for their communities. A man casts his fishing net into the sea, a group of people herd their cattle, a neighbourhood team plays basketball...

Containing over 100 high-quality colour photographs by UK-based photographers Jeremy Hartley, Jenny Matthews, Keith Bernstein, Nancy Durrell-McKenna, John Tordai, Julio Etchart and Philip Wolmuth, and from Asia, Shahidul Alam and Rajendra Shaw, the book offers a unique insight into the lives of people with whom Oxfam works all over the world. *Oxfam 50: Our World in Photographs* is a celebration of the quiet victories in remote places that often go unrecorded. It is a tribute to the people with whom Oxfam has worked over the last 50 years, as well as a celebration of the nature of Oxfam's work, which seeks to give people hope and dignity, and to provide them with support so that they can make a world of difference to their own lives.

Above: *Actor Colin Skipp of 'The Archers' opening Oxfam's new Wastesaver plant in Huddersfield.*

Left: *This small child was one of the first people to benefit from relief supplies arriving in Greece in 1942.*

Introduction to the Images

What does *Oxfam 50* set out to do?

Oxfam is best known as a disaster-relief agency which responds with emergency aid and supplies at times of crisis. This is partly due to the success of its fund-raising appeals, and also because of the high profile that the media give to the world's disasters. By their very nature, disasters continue to hit the headlines, but images of poverty and starvation which compel our generosity are the extreme, the harrowing reality of what occurs when all else has failed.

Disasters come and go. They monopolize public attention for a short time. We are left with vivid

Above: *Water, supplied and funded by Oxfam, arrives at Seri Bandung village, Sumatra, Indonesia.*

Left: *Oxfam food and clothing is distributed in a refugee settlement in Mozambique.*

images of countries ravaged by disaster and a lasting impression of people in the Third World as passive recipients of aid. Rarely do we hear about the attempts to avert disaster, or the courage and resilience needed to live through a catastrophe.

To coincide with its 50th Anniversary year, Oxfam decided to produce a book of photographs to portray a more realistic picture of life in Third World countries. Instead of focusing on floods, famine and feeding centres, the Anniversary photobook *Oxfam 50* presents the positive side of the development story. We are introduced to some of the people with whom Oxfam works overseas, and have been allowed a privileged insight into their lives.

The photobook reveals a day-to-day world, much like our own, in which people are striving, with limited resources, to make a world of difference to their own lives. We meet Sabjada who, after losing her husband and her home to severe flooding, is now an active member of a women's group and a trained midwife. In Senegal, we spend a day with a pastoral family. We visit Addis Ababa, Ethiopia, where neighbours work together re-building their homes, running a community centre and setting up small businesses. In South India, once-nomadic gypsies have opted for a settled life and are learning agricultural skills. In Magsaysay, a suburb of Manila, Philippines, people who work on the municipal rubbish dump are rediscovering traditional skills in healthcare ...

A common theme that emerges in all the photographs, and indeed in all of Oxfam's work, is the people's determination to work for a fairer world and to create a better life for themselves and their families. In the Dominican Republic, where a plan to beautify the capital Santa Domingo threatens many thousands of homes, the residents have started a campaign to fight for their rightful compensation and new homes. In the Philippines, where the livelihoods of fishing communities on Laguna Lake have been all but destroyed to make way for a massive industrial development, people are standing up for their rights and highlighting the environmental implications of the death of the largest inland lake in the world.

How were the projects selected?

In 50 years, Oxfam has established a unique photographic library which provides a compelling visual history of Oxfam and its work with people in developing countries. While staff and project partners now often carry a camera, on occasions Oxfam also commissions professional photographers to work in particular countries.

Over the years, Oxfam has built up good relationships with professional photographers who have chosen, out of solidarity with poor people, to focus their skills on development. In 1991, Oxfam commissioned several of them to visit a range of countries and to provide images of the current overseas programme for use in Oxfam's Anniversary year.

Given that Oxfam now works in over 75 countries and funds over 2,800 long-term development projects, it would have been impossible to include all aspects of the work of our project partners. So began a process of selection, to assess which countries would give a good overall representation of our work. Ten countries were eventually chosen.

The choice of projects was then dependent upon the availability of the photographers and their freedom to work and travel in a particular country in safety, sometimes travelling with local Oxfam staff. The projects were often remote and involved a considerable amount of travel. We asked the photographers to spend at least a day with selected projects, to get to know some of the people, and to capture on film the variety, detail and rich tapestry of everyday life in a developing country.

The countries and projects are diverse. A kindergarten is part of a complex of projects in the Negev Desert, Israel. In Ecuador, Julio Etchart was invited to spend four days in Simiarug, a remote Andean village, and photographed their bi-lingual school. Nancy Durrell-McKenna visited a traditional health-care programme on Manila's main rubbish dump, while Jenny Matthews travelled around Uganda where she witnessed the rebuilding of communities shattered by civil war, the work with people psychologically affected by the war, and Uganda's new war against AIDS.

Oxfam's support for income generation is reflected in the work of Rajendra Shaw who focused on a newly-settled community of gypsies earning money from the sale of bead necklaces in Tamil Nadu, South India, and a small fishing village which has joined with similar villages to form a federation to help them market their catch more profitably.

Poverty is getting worse, not better

These photographs illustrate people's attempts to tackle the obstacles that stand in the way of long-term sustainable development. But most of the people here face an uphill struggle.

The twentieth century will be remembered as a period of great progress and achievement. Enormous strides have been made in health care and education, and new technology has transformed our planet and changed our environment irrevocably. Nevertheless, one in five of the world's population, one billion people, are still unable to afford the basic necessities of life.

Poverty is on the increase for many reasons:

* Rich countries with 25 per cent of the world's population consume 80 per cent of its resources.

* On average the top industrial nations allocate 0.36 per cent of their GNP to overseas development. They spend 20 times this amount on defence.

* Aid to most developing countries remains at inadequate levels. Too much of the aid that is given goes to inappropriate projects.

As a consequence:

* In 1989, developing countries paid $52 billion more to the rich world in debt repayments and interest than it received in aid and new loans.

* The prices of commodities such as tea and coffee, on which poor countries depend for their export earnings, have steadily declined, until in April 1991 they reached their lowest point ever.

* The standard of living for most people in the developed world increased by 20 per cent in the 1980s. For most of the world's poor, living standards fell by the same amount during this time.

* A child dies every 2.4 seconds from hunger or hunger-related diseases.

* A person can expect to reach the age of 75 in the UK and Ireland. In sub-Saharan Africa, life expectancy is 50 years.

* In the world's poorest countries, only 36 per cent have access to safe drinking water.

* 110 million children in the Third World go without basic education. In sub-Saharan Africa, the number of children attending school declined in the 1980s.

Relief supplies are unloaded in Cambodia after the overthrow of Pol Pot's regime in October 1979.

* In 1988 alone, there were over 14 million refugees in the world, 80 per cent of them women.

* In 1950, only one Third World city had a population of over five million. It is estimated that there will be 45 of these huge cities in the developing world by the year 2000.

* In Manila, Philippines, only 12 per cent of the urban population can afford to buy or rent a house or flat. In Mexico City, 60 per cent lives in illegal shanty towns. Half the population of Calcutta lives in overcrowded inner-city slums.

* Environmental damage caused by the pursuit of short-term economic gain is more extreme in the most vulnerable regions of the world, causing rapid depletion of essential natural resources on which poor people depend.

Oxfam's small-scale community approach cannot, of course, tackle the structural causes of poverty but, as you will see in the photographs which follow, often all that people need is a small injection of money, training or equipment to open the doors to development.

What's it like to live in poverty?

Whereas industrial societies in the developed world can provide a safety net, however inadequate, for people who fall below the poverty line, the poorest of the poor in the Third World have no such provision. Without welfare support, family credit, access to health care and education, they spend their lives trying to survive. For them, the implications of long-term poverty are more far-reaching.

Christina's story

After three years of alternating drought and flooding, the once lush and fruitful district of Chama in Zambia is now a virtual wasteland. There is no more game to hunt, and it is impossible to grow maize, the staple crop. For the poorest members of the community, times are desperate.

'We sometimes go without a meal for days; mangoes and wild okra are all there is to eat,' says Christina Ngulube, whose husband left the area four years ago to seek work. The nearest food depot is three days' walk away. Christina takes one of her six children with her, doing odd jobs on the way in return for a meal. She and two friends pool their meagre resources to buy a bag of maize meal between them. There is no money for the children to attend school.

Christina believes that many of her problems could be solved by the construction of a road to her isolated village, so that food could be transported more easily. But this would be a massive project, beyond the means of Zambia's economy.

Millions of poor people around the world face similar problems. The underlying features of poverty are the same: lack of access to essentials like food, clean water, land; poor health care or educational facilities; physical isolation, powerlessness and extreme vulnerability to adversity. All these different aspects combine to create a chain of circumstances from which it becomes increasingly hard to break out.

In Oxfam's experience, development which puts people in charge of their own future offers the best possibility of real and lasting change. Successful development projects aim to build communities' confidence and ability to identify problems – and implement solutions – themselves.

Zamrun's story

In 1984, Zamrun and her husband, Zekander Ali, owned five acres of land, more than enough to support them in fertile Bangladesh. But then the river changed course and washed their land and their livelihood away. The family fled to an embankment where they set up home, marginalized and vulnerable, without the resources of previous years to rebuild after the floods.

After severe flooding in 1989, Zamrun and her family were desperate. They had no more resources on which to draw. Flood waters had eroded the embankment upon which their tiny house stood and had swamped the surrounding agricultural land. For Zekander Ali, who earned subsistence wages on someone else's land, there was no work. Without work there would be no food. The family was once again dependent upon relief. It was then that Zamrun and others came into contact with Own

Harrowing a paddyfield before irrigating and planting. The flood-prevention embankment means that the crop will probably survive the cyclone season.

Village Advancement (OVA), a local organization funded by Oxfam. Abdullah, an OVA worker, encouraged people to organize into small groups to explore alternatives to the yearly cycle of dependence on relief aid. Zamrun's group pooled their resources and established a savings fund to provide capital for small money-making ventures like goat rearing and fruit-tree cultivation. Zamrun saved two takas (worth about four pence) of rice a week and contributed the money to the fund.

Land is the single most important asset in countries like Bangladesh; without it, a person becomes reliant on others for work and wages, and is open to exploitation. New land is constantly being formed in Bangladesh from silt that washes into the Bay of Bengal. By law, this is set aside for the landless, but in practice it is often appropriated by landlords. After advice from OVA about land claims, several small groups joined together in a federation to press for their right to land.

A year later, after more serious flooding, Oxfam representatives returned to the area. The situation was markedly different from the year before. Loans from the savings fund enabled local people to buy enough food to see them through the crisis period. There was a general mood of optimism.

Cutting out the middlemen

Coffee is the Dominican Republic's second-largest export crop, and all of it is produced by small-scale farmers. Traditionally, they have been at the mercy of middlemen, who control access to the markets and to credit for seeds, tools and fertilizers.

'We work from seven in the morning to five in the afternoon. But coffee doesn't bring the farmer much profit,' says José Rodriguez from the Federation of Coffee Farmers' Associations of Bani. 'The benefits of the coffee go to the middlemen. They cheat on the value of the product. Then there are the taxes. We, the small coffee growers, produce the national wealth, but we don't have health centres, schools, roads or bridges, much less a chemist or a doctor.'

An essential element of Oxfam's approach to development is bringing people together. Through better organization, people have more chance of being heard and of solving their own problems.

Oxfam-backed co-operatives have joined forces with others to obtain cheap credit, share storage and processing facilities, and develop a marketing strategy that will allow them to bypass the middlemen. By 1988, these co-ops had gained control of 10 per cent of the country's export trade.

Vulnerability to disasters

Poor people in the Third World have developed survival skills that people in the industrialized North have lost or forgotten. In Vietnam, when Typhoon Becky destroyed houses, crops and livestock in 1990, the people of Ky Anh reacted with great courage and resilience. Storm-whipped waves lashed the shoreline and broke through the sea dyke that had been painstakingly built by the people to protect their livelihoods.

The people of Ky Anh had no recourse to insurance. Damage to the paddy fields would mean no rice and no food unless the crop could be salvaged and the land treated with lime to restore its fertility. Oxfam's country representative was present in Ky Anh during the typhoon. The people started to rebuild their damaged sea dykes almost immediately. There was no time to sit around. The paddy fields were flooded with brackish sea water. The damage caused by the storm had to be rectified so that crops could be replanted and life could return to normal.

Urgent repairs began immediately, and Oxfam staff worked with district officials and engineers in Hanoi to assess ways of improving the dyke. A crash construction programme, involving 3,000 local people and nine bulldozers every day for six months, should ensure that the dyke resists future onslaught from the sea.

Conclusion

Oxfam does not have the resources to eradicate world poverty, but it is helping to change by example through promoting and supporting the kind of sustainable grassroots development which can establish a process that builds on and develops people's initiative and self-confidence.

The title of this book was to have been A World of Difference, but this would have reinforced the sense of difference at the expense of common experience. Oxfam 50 reflects the achievements of Oxfam's partners as they struggle to improve their own lives and illustrates the importance of Oxfam supporters in the process ... and the extent to which they both have helped to make a world of difference to people's lives in their support for a fairer and more sustainable world.

This book is as much a tribute to the people with whom Oxfam has worked over the years, as a celebration of the nature of Oxfam's work which helps people to put their ideas into practice.

LAGUNA BAY

'If you were industrious and had the will to sustain your family, all you had to do was get on to the lake and harness its bounty'. So says Lupo Masaclao, one of the fishermen from Laguna Lake. This lake, the largest area of inland water in Asia, once provided the livelihood for 11,000 families. Now they have to borrow money for food. Disaster struck in 1983 when the lake's only link with other water was closed to provide hydroelectric power for massive industrial development in Metro Manila, built to earn foreign currency to enable the Philippines government pay off its huge external debt. With no government support or compensation, local organizations (with the support of Oxfam) are helping the lakeside communities explore and develop new ways of making a living – from shoe making and tailoring to duck rearing and vegetable growing.

Above: Although these families earn only 50 - 120 pesos (£1.50 - £2.80) in a good month, they are determined to continue fishing. Building a new 'barca' (boat) is a family affair – with neighbours giving helpful advice!

Left: Some of the families who earn a living by fishing are now looking for a new livelihood. Keeping ducks for egg production is one possibility, although it is costly to set up. Ducks cost 60 pesos (£1.40) each, they lay eggs for two years and are then sold for meat at 30 pesos. They don't lay eggs during the wet season (June to August) but still need feeding. Eggs sell at about two pesos each.

Above: Fisher-families have many expenses with the upkeep of the boats and equipment. There are always nets to be mended and, like everything else, the price of nylon twine always goes up – never down.

Right: Five in the morning, returning from the night's fishing. Once they would have expected a catch to include as many as 26 varieties of fish, now there are only three or four. By the year 2000 the lake will have no fish at all if drastic action is not taken.

Right: *The whole family has a part to play. The men catch the fish, the women and children clean, dry and sell. Tessie is laying out Ayungín and Biya, two of the varieties that survive. The family will earn between 30 and 50 pesos a day from selling dried fish.*

AGRICULTURE & CROPS

For generations, the world's poorest farmers have been coaxing a living from the land. Their knowledge and skills are immense but, even so, they live on a knife-edge. It's not unusual to lose one harvest to disease or drought and most can survive – just. But if the next harvest fails... and the next... they may have to eat the grain they were saving to sow next year or lose their land and turn to casual labour at starvation wages. Often very little is needed to break out of the poverty trap; a loan for a new plough or irrigation, at rates they can afford, or training to cope with a changing environment. Many groups of landless labourers, usually the poorest of the poor, are also helped by Oxfam to gain legal title to land and bring wasteland into cultivation.

Above: *Over 80 per cent of the population of Ethiopia depends on agriculture for its survival.*

Right: *Women are responsible for growing 80 per cent of the food produced in sub-Saharan Africa.*

Above: *High in the mountains of Vietnam, this Hmong farmer is making the most of the breeze to winnow his rice crop.*

Below: Women near San Juan in Ecuador work idle land they are reclaiming under land reform laws.

Above: *These terraced hillsides in the Philippines make the best use of limited space.*

Left: *Red chilli peppers drying in the sun on Hatiya Island, Bangladesh.*

Above: *In the Sa Pa district of Vietnam, the whole family works together harvesting their rice crop.*

Below: *Some Bedouin families in the Negev, Israel, still depend on their flocks for milk, meat and wool.*

A PASTORALIST PROJECT IN SENEGAL

L'Association pour le Développement de Namarel is a non-governmental organization set up by 17 groups of Pulaar pastoralists in the semi-arid Ferlo region of Northern Senegal. The Association aims to involve its members in projects which improve the lives of the people and their animals, their most important asset.

So far ADENA has organized training for veterinary auxiliaries and literacy classes. It is establishing cereal banks – which buy surplus grain at fair prices when there is a good harvest, and re-sell it during years of poor harvests at equally fair prices, helping to avoid the huge price swings in the markets. Their next projects are to improve people's health by up-grading water supplies and providing community health care.

Above: *The men of Mewell village meet to discuss the digging of a new well. There are important issues at stake – who will have access to it; who will dig it; what contribution can the villagers make and who will look after it.*

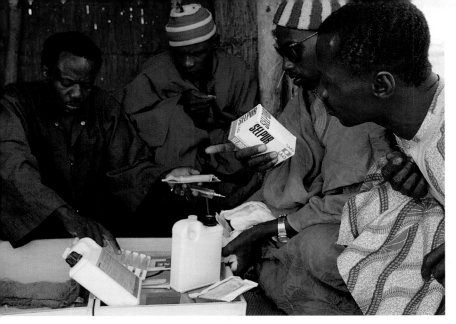

Above and right: *Kibiri is the local auxiliary vet trained to vaccinate cattle, and to recognize and treat the most common diseases. Livestock equals wealth in this area of Senegal, so it's important to have healthy animals and to prevent outbreaks of disease.*

Left and below: The women of Mewell village discussing the practicalities of setting up a cereal 'bank' with Mariam Dem, Oxfam's Project Officer. Although the Pulaar are mainly pastoralists, they also grow millet – which they eat as cous cous. The women feel a cereal bank will be a great help to them in years when the harvest fails.

A PASTORALIST FAMILY

Kibiri and his family are pastoralists, that is, people who make a living from keeping animals. They live in an area where the rains are often too erratic and unreliable to be able to grow crops, but when there is enough rain they grow a crop of millet or sorghum. Kiribi, his wife and children live with his father, and his brother's family. This means they have all the skilled labour they need for herding, milking, dairy processing and growing crops. The men and older boys can go away for several weeks at a time, following the rains with their herds to areas of new pasture.

As well as all the domestic chores, the women and girls are responsible for the old, sick and new-born animals too weak or small to move with the herds. The women make yoghurt from surplus milk, which they sell or barter for oil, salt and other household goods.

Right and below right: Collecting water from the well. So that she need make only two trips a day, Kibiri's wife persuades her daughters to help.

Below: Ousman (Kibiri) Ba's household in Tekkangel village.

Left: *Preparing and cooking meals can take a lot of time – but you're never too young to learn! Kibiri's wife is teaching her daughters how to make a stew, which will be eaten with cous cous.*

Right: *The Pulaar think blackened gums, lips and chin very attractive. They use a powder made from groundnuts roasted to 'charcoal'.*

Below: When the cows are milked, the calf is tied to its mother's foreleg. To leave plenty for the calf, only a small amount of milk is taken.

Above: Every day the cattle, sheep and goats are taken to the 'forage' to drink. When your livestock are your bank account, you look after them well.

DAKAR – SENEGAL

In Dakar, the Oxfam Project Officer, Mariam Dem, concentrates on work with women's groups, people with disabilities and vocational training for young people. Oxfam offers popular small-scale, flexible credit-funding to groups who show great determination to succeed in their ventures and to make the repayments.
A small amount of interest is charged, the capital is repaid to Oxfam and the interest paid into the group's bank account. This accustoms the group to using banks, teaches them that borrowing money 'costs' money, and provides capital for the future.
Mariam is encouraging the groups to form a federation to strengthen their autonomy and to improve their bargaining power with local banks.

Below: *The Association Sénégalaise d'Aide à l'Insertion des Necessiteux, is a training centre for young people. As in many other cities, it is hard to get a job if you have no skills. Here they learn how to be carpenters, mechanics, secretaries and electricians.*

Above: *The students learn practical and theoretical work. A carpentry class is making furniture.*

Left: *Many of the students set up their own workshops once they have finished their training. This metal-worker is making a children's slide.*

Above and right: *In Le Marché Cambérène you will find the Groupement des Femmes de Parcelles Assainies. These women are funded by Oxfam to set up in business. Some are tailors, others have market stalls selling a wide variety of goods ranging from clothes, fish and vegetables, to spices and tea.*

STREET SCENES

For visitors and tourists, markets are fascinating and exciting places, full of colour, noise and bustle, new sights and scents. These are where we find our souvenirs to remind us of holidays or business trips.

In rural areas they are not just places to sell surplus produce and buy domestic goods, they are important social gathering-places as well. For poor people without television, radio or telephones, or for those from remote communities, market day provides an opportunity to meet friends and relations, to exchange the latest family news, to find someone to write or read a letter, to find a job, to find a craftsman, or hear the latest song. For those living around the marketplace it provides endless entertainment watching the comings and goings!

Left: *A derelict mansion, once owned by ex-dictator Trujillo, in Santo Domingo (Dominican Republic) has been taken over by squatter families, desperate for somewhere to live.*

Left: In Senegal, as in many other African countries, the majority of trading in markets is done by women. In households headed by women, it is their only income.

Below: Women are in charge of selling the fish caught in Laguna Bay in the Philippines.

Above: *One of the women's groups,
funded by Oxfam in Dakar, Senegal,
selling fresh vegetables.*

Below: Grinding fresh coconut in Manila, Philippines.

Above: Market day gives people from remote villages a chance to exchange news with friends and relatives.

Left: In Uganda the whole family goes to market; you're never too young to help.

Right: *In the Sa Pa province of Vietnam, the majority of people are illiterate. The market is a useful place if you need to find someone to write a letter or read the latest newspaper.*

Below: *Carmen Miranda, Senegal style! A useful way to advertise your goods.*

LAQIYA – ISRAEL

Oxfam is involved with the Bedouin population of the Negev within the borders of Israel, the poorest community in the country. Many families have been deprived of their flocks and grazing lands, and live in small communities in tin shacks.

In 1989 the Israeli government agreed that Laqiya could be a permanent place of habitation. The tin shacks are being replaced as families save enough money to build new cement and stone houses. Oxfam has worked with the community of Laqiya since 1981 on health, water supplies and pre-school education. A local association, also funded by Oxfam, has started kindergartens in several Bedouin communities. These provide an important start for children where education is limited.

Above: *Some Bedouin families still keep herds of goats and sheep – but in far smaller numbers now that access to grazing areas is restricted.*

Overleaf: *The settlement of Laqiya. For over 20 years the local people have lived in small 'illegal' shacks, built without licence and liable to demolition by the authorities.*

Right: *An initiative in Laqiya has been to revitalize traditional weaving. New designs are being developed, based on traditional techniques, and new markets sought for the rugs produced.*

Right: Some children take a snack to school to eat at mid-morning.

Left: *Laqiya 'New Town'. Gradually, new stone and concrete houses are appearing, built a bit at a time as money is saved each year.*

Below: *Access to education for Bedouin children has been limited. Schools are provided by the government but the quality of teaching is poor.*
The Educational Association of Negev trains pre-school teachers, runs pre-schools and encourages parents to take an active interest in their children's school work.

ADULTS

People speak to us first through the way they look. Faces can reveal a lot about the inner strength and character of a person and their life. Clothes are significant too; they mark out rich from poor, the rulers from the ruled, women from men. They show the kinds of work we do, the climate we live in and our culture.

No matter how poor, and how difficult their lives, most people take pride in their appearance. Efforts are made to keep everyday clothes clean. Traditional costumes and jewellery are stored with care and brought out for special occasions. With increased tourism and travel our own fashions reflect ethnic designs, fashions and fabrics from cultures thousands of miles away.

Right: In Ecuador, extremes of daily temperature make lots of layers the easiest way to cope. Hats are essential at high altitudes to keep off the sun.

Left: Washing day in the mountains of the Dominican Republic.

Above: *Exhausted after a street parade in Ecuador!*

Left: *One of the tribal elders from Bonaue – one of the 'viewpoints' looking over the mountains of Luzon, Philippines. The elders dress in their finery, and charge tourists to photograph them. A useful way of earning some money when you are too old to work!*

Right: *The Coptic Church plays an important role in many people's lives in Ethiopia.*

Above: *Traditional fabrics and modes of dress give way to mass-produced cloth and styles even in remote pastoralist communities in Senegal.*

Right: *Your produce has to be fresh to get the best prices in the market – even if it means getting up at dawn, as here at Santa Rosa in the Philippines.*

ADDIS ABABA – ETHIOPIA

Addis Ababa and other cities are not immune to the after-effects of war or to depressed world prices of coffee, Ethiopia's main export. Refugees from war zones and farmers whose land was confiscated under Haile Selassie have flocked to the cities. Unemployment is high and there are shortages of basic goods. The World Bank is now willing to give Ethiopia loans but it insists on 'structural adjustment'. This means lifting food-subsidies, which puts most food beyond the pockets of the poor, like the inhabitants of Kebele 29, where Oxfam works. Oxfam's Integrated Urban Project is helping to combat poverty and poor living conditions. Hygienic latrines, communal kitchens and a recreation centre have been built and small loans are being made.

Right: 798 families live in Kebele 29, 30 per cent of which are headed by women.

Above: Over 130 people are members of the community savings and loan scheme. Sixty people have already received loans to help them set up businesses. The most popular are grain marketing, trading and brewing. These women are drying hops ready for making beer.

Right: Sixty kitchens and 33 toilets have been built so far – and more are on the way. There are always people ready to help.

Left: *133 houses have been targeted for immediate help, so far 44 houses have been rebuilt. Imagine the joy of pulling down your old house, knowing your new one will be ready tomorrow!*

Below: *The new community centre provides a focus for Kebele 29. Meetings and parties are held here, and friends meet to drink coffee and chat or play table-tennis.*

A SEA COAL FAMILY

Nery Medina is a member of the Kennel Women's group in Lota. It was started in 1986, and really took off in 1987 with support from Oxfam. To earn money, the women have workshops where they learn how to embroider and make stuffed toys. They are encouraged to find communal solutions to problems and to share resources. Nery and her neighbour, for example, run a bakery. Meetings also give women the chance to discuss common issues and share their concerns; domestic life, sexual relations, abortion, domestic violence. These help them to develop more self-confidence; they know they are not alone. They campaign on these issues and have a regular slot on local radio to keep the community informed, and they put pressure on policy-makers, both local and national, to take women's issues seriously.

Nery enjoys the meetings; apart from anything else they give her a chance just to sit and chat with her friends – a break from her tough life as a sea-coaler.

Above: '*Chinchoreras*' (*sea-coalers*) *at work on the shore of the beach at Pueblo Hundido, where the sea washes up the thin black powder discharge from the coal mine.*

Above: Nery Medina comes to Pueblo Hundido ('sunken village') every other day to collect coal. She uses some of it at home and sells the rest.

Left: 'I used to go into the sea to collect the coal but two women died last year – one drowned and one got pneumonia, so now I collect what I can from the beach.'

t: Nery and a neighbour carrying
s of coal dust back to Lota, a round-
of eight miles.

ow left: Once home, the coal is
d, bagged and sold for 80 pesos
out 13 pence) for a 50-kilo bag.

ow: One of Killen's initiatives is to
ourage women to share resources.
y has a bread oven, so now she and
eighbour bake 120 loaves of bread
ry other day. They keep some for
r families, the rest they sell to
hbours.

FOOD, PREPARATION & COOKING

The world produces more than enough food for everyone, but tonight 700 million people will go to sleep hungry. Rapid population-growth, sometimes blamed for hunger and malnutrition in developing countries, is part of the problem.

Yet between 1950 and 1986 world production of grain increased by 220 per cent, far outpacing population growth. Floods, drought and other natural disasters can also contribute to food shortages. But what really makes people vulnerable is poverty. People go hungry because they do not have money to buy food, or land on which to grow it. In the long term, hunger can only be solved by changing the political and economic policies that cause poverty.

Above: *When you visit a Bedouin household in Laqiya, coffee is always served. The ritual of making coffee, roasting and grinding the beans, symbolises hospitality and welcome.*

Right: *Cooking Mandazi, a popular dish in Uganda, made from deep-fried mashed bananas and flour.*

Above: *Pastoralist families in Senegal eat meat only when there are guests to feed. In this case, the photographer!*

Right: *If you don't need a whole pineapple in the markets of Manila, Philippines, you can buy as much, or as little, as you want.*

Left: In Tamil Nadu, India, most families eat rice three times a day, sometimes with vegetable curry, or just with salt and chillies.

Above: The ugali – made from cassava or maize flour – is put in to a basket and everyone helps themselves. In Uganda the ugali is eaten either with soup, as here, or meat stew.

Left: Fish, shellfish and sea urchins like these are becoming a rare sight in the sea around Pueblo Hundido in Chile, because of pollution.

COPADEPA – DOMINICAN REPUBLIC

In the Dominican Republic a lively campaign is being waged. Fifty thousand families are threatened by plans to 'beautify' their city. Homes painstakingly constructed and cared for are being bulldozed. New homes are promised but rarely materialize; those that do are 20 km from the city, breaking community ties and separating families. All to make way for a lighthouse to commemorate Columbus – and the tourists who will visit it. A local organization, COPADEPA, works with community groups throughout Santo Domingo to help residents organize their campaign. Oxfam provided money for them to produce booklets and a slide show. In this way communities learn more about the plans for their areas and how they can contribute ideas and, perhaps, save their homes.

Left: The sign reads 'Just and humane removal' - one of the many signs and posters which appeared during the campaign as local residents got together to protect themselves. They are not against improving the city. 'But isn't it possible', they ask, 'to have urban renewal in which the knowledge and contribution of those affected can be creatively united with those of the government?'

Right: El faro de Colon – the Columbus lighthouse – into which massive resources have been poured. If the lighthouse is ever switched on the electricity needed will put lights out all over Santo Domingo.

Right: *A family sitting in the ruins of their family home in Villa Duarte. The government dumps the 'desalojos' in Panto, a site 20 km outside the city - where there are no building materials and no work or transport.*

Below: *A demonstration by 'desalojos', who have received no compensation, at a ceremony during which President Belagner handed out keys to new flats built on the site of their demolished homes. The demonstrators claimed the keys were given to party supporters, not to 'desalojos'.*

FAIRER SHARES FOR COFFEE GROWERS?

'We, the small coffee-growers, produce wealth but we have nothing which permits us to l
like human beings. We don't have medical centres, schools, roads, much less a chemist
or a doctor. Food is at paupers level, even though we produce the wealth. Of every
100 pesos, we lose around 46. But here at the co-op it's different. The benefits go to the
farmer, not the merchant.' José is a member of the Nucleus of Coffee Farmers of Bani.
Most coffee in the Dominican Republic is produced by small farmers. They are pooling
their resources and marketing direct to the export trade. The nuclei have formed
a federation so the farmers have access to warehousing, processing and cheap credit.
For José, and many like him, this is a step towards realizing his dreams of health care,
schooling for his children and electricity.

Above: A poster showing the factors influencing farmers' lives: such as government policies; structural adjustment imposed by the IMF, banks, moneylenders and middlemen.

Left: Coffee is their main cash-crop, but the farmers of El Cacao also grow maize and beans as food crops.

Below: A meeting of La Esperanza, the coffee-growers association in El Cacao.

RELAXING

Despite the struggle and hardships of life in poor communities, people still manage to find time to meet friends and relax. Most of us, in our spare time, switch on the TV; when you don't have one it's more fun to get together with your neighbours. In many countries poetry, stories and songs are not just entertainment, but keep alive history and culture, and spread news and social comment.

Some of the games we play originated in Third World countries – as did kite-flying, spreading across Asia and Europe along the ancient trade routes from China.

Many pastimes are common throughout the world; card games are as popular in South India and Ecuador as in the Philippines.

***Left and below:** In villages in Uganda music is always live! Musicians are welcomed at important social occasions like weddings. Music and song are a powerful form of expression everywhere. They also help spread messages about important social issues.*

Above: *A card school in Santo Roas, Philippines. Tessie and her friends enjoy the occasional break from daily routine.*

Below: *Good wind, high altitude and open spaces make kite flying a popular family pastime in Ecuador.*

POST CYCLONE IN BANGLADESH

On 30th April 1992 the worst cyclone for over a decade hit the south-east coast of Bangladesh. Within hours an estimated 150,000 people were dead and four million homeless. Large parts of the mainland and several islands were under water. Hatiya and Nijhum Dwip are little more than sandbars. Those who can afford it build their houses on raised earth-mounds and embankments, but three-quarters of the population had no such protection. Dwip Unnayan Sangstha, a local organization supported by Oxfam, concentrated its relief efforts on these people. DUS assessed the damage and identified the most vulnerable families, who were then helped by DUS to form groups to share their meagre resources and pool their labour.

Above: *Once the cyclone passed the survivors set about putting together a shelter against the rain and wind using whatever could be salvaged.*

Above: *Boats leave Jahamara Ghat for Nijhum Dwip (Islands of Silence) carrying cattle, chickens, bamboo, tree saplings, baskets, some of the many things that have to be bought on the mainland.*

Below: *Rebuilding is a community effort in Shagoria village, Hatiya Island. Here a timber frame for a new thatched roof is being made.*

Left: There are few signs to show that Hatiya Island was once heavily populated. Until the flood waters recede every high tide brings more problems.

Below: Hafez Mahubur is a respected elder of his village. He was lucky; he had the resources to rebuild his home. He has also spent time and energy sheltering and helping his less fortunate neighbours.

A DAY IN THE LIFE OF SABJADA

Sabjada Begum is a widow raising her son and daughters on her own. She has lost her home five times through erosion but, thanks to Dwip Unnayan Sangstha, her future is secure. Many people living in Hatiya have come from the mainland in search of new land in the delta. DUS was formed in 1982 to help the landless stand up for their rights against rich landowners. Oxfam has funded DUS since 1985 and its work has expanded to include a savings and loan scheme and training projects. Sabjada has trained as a midwife. Forging strong communities which can work together on common problems has changed life for many on Hatiya and Nijhum Dwip. As we have seen, without DUS the effects of the latest cyclone would have taken much longer to recover from.

Right: Occasionally Sabjada buys 'muri' (puffed rice) dipped in gur (date-palm syrup), made by one of her neighbours. It makes a delicious treat.

Left: Like all parents Sabjada helps her children get ready for school. She takes great pride in the fact that her daughter is doing well at school.

Above: *Sabjada and her friends run a small business. They buy paddy and then process it – parboil, dry and husk – so it is ready for sale to other families in the area.*

Below: Sabjada buys milk every day as she doesn't own a cow or buffalo.

Below: *Sabjada is the general secretary of her local women's group. They meet every week to discuss and work out solutions to common problems.*
Last year DUS helped them to get two acres of land They are discussing what to plant and where to sell the produce.

Left: *Hasna Ara Begum and her new son. Sabjada is a volunteer midwife, trained by DUS, and is using her new skills for the benefit of the village. It's aways nice to see a successful result!*

Below: *Once the children are in bed Sabjada has a chance to relax.*

DYKE-BUILDING IN VIETNAM

'There was a mighty wind and the sea started to rise – within half an hour everywhere was flooded. All we could do was to pick up our children and set out into the darkness. I forced my way through water that was up to my neck, carrying our two boys who were crying in terror.' This is Nguyen Can Tu's description of the night typhoon Becky hit Ky Ahh province of Vietnam. The people of Ky Ahh are used to typhoons and the havoc they wreak. Seawater flooding leaves the coastal land full of salt, which means low yields for crops and food shortages for the province. What Tu and his fellow villagers needed was a better dyke. Engineers from Hanoi Water Resources University and Oxfam visited the site and drew up a new, stronger dyke design.

Above: *Local technicians and team leaders were trained in basic construction techniques. Then 3,000 people, assisted by nine bulldozers, set to work on the 17km long embankment.*

Below: *Soil was collected in baskets from nearby fields and carried to the site to be compacted by machines. The inner slope was planted with grass, and the seaward slope covered with large, carefully placed rocks, to protect it from the battering of the waves.*

Right: *Less than a year later, after about a million days of work by local people, the new dyke was completed, ready to protect the livelihood of 5,000 families from the worst effects of future typhoons.*

WATER & ITS USES

A family of six needs over 20 gallons of water a day for drinking, cooking and washing. But only one in three of the world's households has a water supply at home. Most others get their water from rivers, lakes, springs or wells, or, in towns, from standpipes shared with hundreds of other families. Throughout the world's poorest countries women damage their health and spend hours every day carrying huge containers of water, often from sources several miles away. To sink a well or pipe water from a spring and maintain the system, people need access to land with a water source, to capital, to equipment and know-how. Oxfam helps communities find the solutions which will work best for them – and which will keep working.

Right: Washing in the street in the Zona Colonial in Santo Domingo. Continuous power cuts mean that water cannot be pumped into the houses.

Left: In Uganda, Oxfam is working with rural communities to upgrade water sources like this. Improving access to water, and its quality, keeps people healthy.

Left: Clean water is important to fishermen too. Their livelihood vanishes with the fish when lakes, rivers and shorelines become polluted.

Right: In South India wells can be many metres deep. When the water table is high, after the monsoon, collecting water doesn't involve quite such a climb.

FESTIVALS, RITUALS

Rituals, ceremonies and festivals play an important role in all our lives, whether marking family occasions: birth, marriage, death; religious events like Christmas or Holi; or celebrating the start of a new year or a good harvest. They are the 'glue' that helps bind families and communities.

In rural communities the year revolves around the growing season, each point in the agricultural cycle marked with village festivals. The New Year is celebrated in many parts of the world and gives people the chance to visit relatives and friends, eat special foods, and to have a break before facing the challenge of another year. Economic poverty, however, is by no means an indication of poverty in other areas of life.

Above and right: Meskel is an important day for Coptic Christians in Ethiopia. Celebrated in September, Meskel commemorates the finding of the 'true cross'. The day starts early with readings and prayers led by the priests and dignitaries in their finest robes.

Above: A funeral feast for the villagers of Muntyean in the Philippines. All the friends, relatives and neighbours visit the family to offer support, and are fed the traditional meal of boiled rice and pork. After five days the body is transferred into the final coffin – a hewn-out tree trunk – and placed in the tomb.
Then the guests leave and the family and village elders sit together in silence, watching and listening for signs that the loved one wants to communicate.
A bird flying into the room, for example, would be interpreted as a sign by the elders.

Right: Some of the villagers of Chowrungi village, Bangladesh are Hindus. Music, singing and dancing play an important role in many of their festivals.

BI-LINGUAL SCHOOL: ECUADOR

The parish of Simiatug extends over a vast area. The mainly indigenous population speaks Quichua rather than Spanish. Many leave the area to escape the problems of poverty and soil erosion only to face equally serious problems of unemployment and homelessness in the cities. In the 1980s a group of local people formed the Fundación Yunacuna Paz Yachana Huasi to tackle the problems of their communities and to develop rural schools. The Fundación has developed materials in Quichua, relevant to the life of the area. They run training courses for teachers; promote improved agriculture methods on school plots and set up libraries. They hope to strengthen local organizations and encourage young people to stay in their communities.

Above: *Picture books are always popular. They are even more fun when you can show off by reading them to your friends!*

Right: *Off to school. Although there is now a school in most communities, it can involve quite a walk for children from the outlying farms.*

Below: *Learning how words are made. Consonants are green, vowels are red.*

Right: *Why should children have all the fun? The Fundación makes sure there is always space and time for the adults to learn too.*

Below: *Teacher Francisco Quisa is paid a stipend by the Fundación until the school is recognised by the state, which will then pay his salary.*

Above: *Quiet reading time! Many of the materials have been developed specially by the Fundación.*

Right: *I've finished my lunch – how much longer till I can go out to play?*

CHILDREN'S PORTRAITS

Children have always helped with family chores. Looking after younger brothers and sisters, fetching firewood and water, helping on the market stall, tending animals and helping with farm work – all are part of growing up. But increasing poverty, caused by debt, migration, the illness or death of an adult breadwinner, can turn children's work into child labour. Childhood should be a happy, secure time. Sadly, for millions of children, life is far from happy. The United Nations Convention on the Rights of the Child states that all children have the right to life, health and education irrespective of race, colour, sex, language or disability. Perhaps it is time for adults, wherever they live, to take responsibility for the world's children. After all, they are our future.

Above: Now that her family live a settled life in Nariodai, this Gypsy child has the chance to go to school.

Left: School dinners in Simiatug, Ecuador.

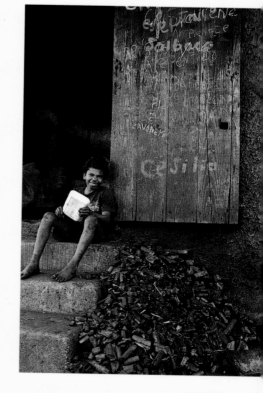

Right: Helping out with the family business selling charcoal in Santo Domingo in the Dominican Republic.

Left: 'Here's looking at you kid!'

Below: In many Third World countries older children are left in charge of their younger siblings, as here in Addis Ababa, Ethiopia.

Above: *Children in the Central Cordillera region of Luzon, Philippines.*

Right: *Basketball is the unofficial national sport of the Philippines.*

Above: *Wrecked cars make great playthings for children in the Negev, Israel.*

AROMA

Five hundred families live on Aroma, the main dump for Metro Manila in the Philippines, and earn a living as scavengers. In Magsaysay, the village around the dump, another 54,000 families live in homes made from scrap materials. Most people have major health problems but nobody has money for medicines or treatment. A group of local women have taken things into their own hands. They make traditional herbal medicines and have organized their own training in basic obstetrics and family planning. With no effective state services to turn to the responsibility for their family's health rests almost entirely on the women. The programme is just a beginning – they are determined to improve their lives and build a better future for their children.

Left: Nanay (Mother) Inding is the Vice Chairperson of the Health Committee. Many of the women have a reputation as rebels with the government and their husbands. In reality they are trying to make a better life for the next generation.

Right: Magsaysay village is built on land owned by the Port Authority. High tides flood much of the area.

Above: *The local women have organized health education classes which are very popular although they are held in less than sanitary conditions.*

Below: *Whole families work on the dump. A family of six earns about 70 pesos (£1.60) a week; barely enough for food when rice costs 10 pesos a kilo and which a family can eat in one meal – just with salt and little else.*

Overleaf: *Plastic bottles and sheeting, scrap metal, tins and bottles are all resold to scrap merchants.*

MAKING AND MOVING

Creativity is not separate from everyday life, it is one of the tools for survival – whether it is employed in making something for yourself or to sell, as therapy, or used for devising a practical solution to a problem. The poorer you are, the more creative you must be. A bicycle is not just transport for one person; it can be loaded with produce and wheeled, it can pull a cart to and from market, it can drive an irrigation system and, when too worn out to mend, can be turned into useful tools and implements, like spinning wheels. People have created a range of uses for the banana plant; the leaves can be used for plates and roofing, the thick stem can be cut and hollowed out into bowls, or chopped up and fed to cattle.

Above: *In poor communities there is rarely money for buying toys, so children make their own. This boy in Uganda is making a ball from banana leaves.*

Left: *One way of getting your produce to market is by bicycle!*

Above: *In the Gypsy settlement at Nariodai, South India, everyone of all ages makes bead necklaces for sale at festivals throughout the region.*

Right: *Making baskets at an occupational therapy centre run by the Medical Foundation of Uganda.*

RE-SETTLING GYPSIES IN SOUTHERN INDIA

There are thought to be between 20,000 and 30,000 Gypsies in Tamul Nadu and Andhra Pradesh. They are distinct from the rest of the population, who view them with suspicion. Traditionally they made a living from hunting, making and selling bead necklaces, herbal medicines and begging. Gradually life became more precarious as dwindling forests made it hard to find animals and medicinal plants. The government allocated deforested land for three settled communities, but gave them no assistance.

CROP helps the Gypsies to improve health care, literacy and farming skills, and to integrate with other communities. They have also helped them form an association for buying beads and copper wire in bulk, and therefore more cheaply.

Above: CROP now works with three Gypsy communities. In Nariodai it has provided wells for drinking water and irrigation – especially useful for Kaapidurais marrow patch!

Left: The communities still rely on bead-necklace making for income – but now they elect people to market the necklaces for the whole group. Paapi is a very successful saleswoman.

Below: The Gypsies are known as 'Narikuravas' – fox hunters. Although many Gypsies are now settled, hunting foxes and wildfowl is still important. They provide both food and talismen (tails and teeth) to sell as lucky charms.

Overleaf: Kaapidurai is still a hunter at heart - but he and the children help Paapi with the agricultural work - as here, treading in 'green' manure. They feel that the settlement, with the nearby school, will provide a more secure future for their children.

A DAY IN THE LIFE OF FISHERMEN IN SOUTHERN INDIA

The fishermen of Manakudy village belong to the Kanya Kumari Fishermen's Federation which is affiliated to the South Indian Fishermen's Association, set up to help the small fishing communities. The Federation helps to build awareness of the fishermen's rights and to assert them against rich fishermen with large mechanised boats. It also ensures a fair price for their catch by conducting the auctions at which they are sold and also makes sure that they receive payment on the same day. This cuts out the delays associated with selling to merchants, who pay a little at a time and keep the fishermen in debt. The Federation sells good quality fishing gear at fair prices and is helping to find ways of preserving fish to get better prices.

Above: Sea fishing in a country boat needs a team of three. The catch is divided into four parts, the fourth share going to the owner of the boat and fishing gear. Shahiraj (on the right) hopes to buy a powerboat soon although it will mean leaving the village to move farther up the coast as the sea here is too rough for powerboats.

Left: Late afternoon in Manakudy village. Once the gear and nets have been mended and a meal cooked and eaten there is time to relax. A group can always be found for playing cards – a pastime almost as popular as a visit to the cinema.

Overleaf: The fishermen go out at 6.30am after some 'Kanji', rice soup. They tie their gear, nets and floats to the boat, and once in calmer water they hoist the sail. Negotiating the waves takes skill, experience and teamwork. They fish all the year round except for a month during the monsoon when the sea is too rough.

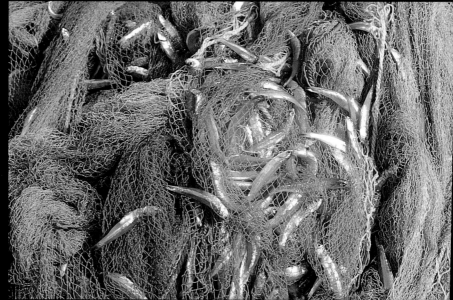

Right: These fishermen catch small anchovy-type fish, mainly for local consumption. Some people, like Sahiraj and his 'team', fish for cuttlefish caught with a hook and line and which sell for around Rs150 (£3) each. They are in great demand for export to Japan.

Left: Once the nets have been hauled in they remove the fish by standing under the net and shaking them out on to the beach.

Below: The fishermen start returning at 11.30 am, and the catch is sold off each boat as it returns. The catch is laid out on the sand, a minimum price is quoted by the auctioneer and the bidding starts.

UGANDA

Armed conflict is both a consequence and cause of poverty in Uganda. Tyranny and factional politics destroyed civil administration, and conflict deepened the divisions in the country and damaged the social fabric of its communities. One of Oxfam's priorities is to help the rehabilitation of communities such as those in Kumi District, and to help develop communications through training and information-exchanges between groups with similar experiences. Health care is another important area of work and involves the training of community-based health-care workers; the development of home-based care for AIDS patients; and the upgrading of water supplies. The greatest threat to Oxfam's work in Uganda is the continuing violence.

Above: Mother and child health-care clinics in Kasese are always well attended.

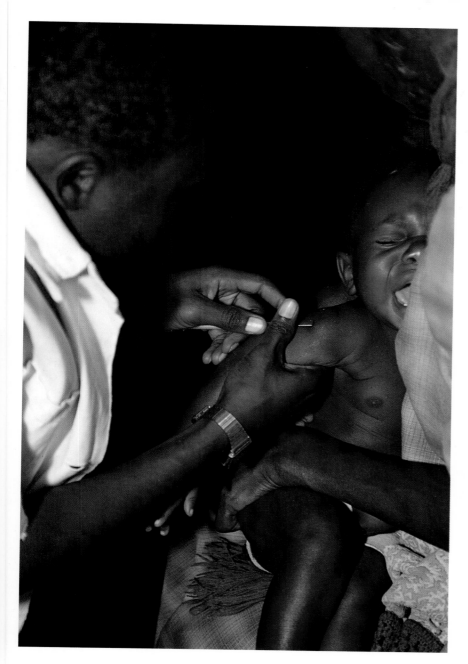

Left: *Mother and child health-care and immunization programmes have a vital role to play in improving health and preventing deaths from childhood diseases.*

Below: *AIDS is a major concern throughout Uganda. This poster is part of a nationwide campaign to alert people to the risks. Oxfam supports the campaign and projects that focus on voluntary home-based support for patients and their families.*

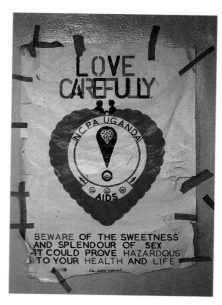

Left: In Kumi, Oxfam's relief and rehabilitation programme was designed to take account of the traditional role of women as the growers of food.
The programme was run, organized and monitored by women. The cassava was Kumi's most important food crop. A disease-resistant strain was introduced and is being collected here.

Below: Ugandans place a high value on education. Since 1980 the number of primary schools has doubled, with communities helping to build them. Lessons started in this village before the school was built.

Above: The Uganda branch of the Medical Foundation for Care of Victims of Torture receives funding from Oxfam, and is one of the few organizations in Africa working to help victims of war trauma and torture.

Left: A stark reminder of the Luwero massacres of 1984. This period of Uganda's history helped define a new role for Oxfam: as witness to major human-rights abuses it determined to take an active role in informing the public and policy-makers of the conditions in which so much of Oxfam's work is carried out.

SUNRISE, SUNSET

However generously the public in developed countries may give in times of emergencies overseas, this will not eliminate world poverty. Nor can the local actions of poor communities, supported by voluntary organizations, alone provide the solution. The growing gap between rich and poor produces ever more suffering, conflict, instability and environmental damage. The high-consuming North cannot expect the South to tackle environmental problems unless it is equally prepared to tackle structural injustices in its relationship with the South. Building a fairer world means taking urgent action in the North to redress the inequality of the global economy which marginalizes and impoverishes so many of the world's inhabitants.

Above: As the sun sets Kaapidurai and his fellow hunters set off for a night's hunting.

Left: For the fishermen of Hatia, the day starts at 4 am. These large fishing boats are expensive and are owned jointly by a group.

Overleaf: The fishermen of Kanya Kumari are up as the sun rises, making ready their boats.

A Brief History of Oxfam

Founding

Oxfam came into being in October 1942, in the middle of a world war. Food scarcity was a major problem, as resources were diverted from food production to fuelling the war economies. By 1940, the German army had overwhelmed much of Europe, and the British government was determined to cut off all possible supply lines to the enemy. Throughout the conflict, the Allies pursued a policy of 'total war' and enforced a rigid blockade against all countries under German occupation.

The country most affected was Greece, which normally imported over half of its food needs.

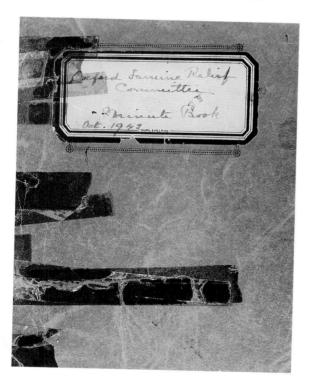

Above: Little did Oxfam's founders dream that the organization they founded in October 1942 would still be in existence in 1992.

Left: A small boy at Mala Camp for displaced people in Zambezia province, Mozambique.

Soon after capitulation in spring 1941, the Greek people began to experience severe food shortages. By September, people were dying in the streets.

The Oxford Committee for Famine Relief

During 1942, eminent figures and citizen groups began to protest against the British commitment to total blockade. They wanted to send 'controlled relief' to Greece and Belgium. Edith Pye, a Quaker with a lifetime's involvement in relief work, was the most active organizer. Her visit to Oxford sparked the formation of the Oxford Committee for Famine Relief in October 1942.

Early in 1943, the Oxford Committee registered as a charity and began fundraising in earnest. An appeal to individuals connected with the university initially raised £3,000. Then, as a result of a strenuous campaign, the people of the city of Oxford followed suit. A Greek Relief Week of lunchtime talks, concerts, slide shows, church events and house-to-house collections raised an impressive £12,700.

Distress in post-war Europe

VE day brought freedom; but the shortages and destruction caused by war continued to inflict suffering throughout Europe for years to come. Although rationing and austerity continued in Britain, many people felt stirred by the suffering on the Continent. All over the country, people collected clothes and sent food parcels to Europe.

The Oxford Committee for Famine Relief mounted a vigorous Appeal for Europe. A shop in Broad Street, Oxford, was opened in 1948 as a collection point for donations (mainly food and clothes) to be sent overseas. The shop, still in use today, became a thriving concern and the first permanent charity shop of its kind. Despite the climate of austerity, the Committee raised £25,000-worth of goods between 1946 and 1948. Oxfam's contribution was dispatched to Europe where it was distributed by church and voluntary groups.

Consolidation

By the late 1940s, the pressing need for post-war relief aid in Europe had declined and a number of relief groups and committees closed down. However, the driving force of Cecil Jackson-Cole, the Oxford eccentric Honorary Secretary, kept the Committee in existence. Due to his enthusiasm and business backing, its operations were extended to include the 'relief of suffering arising as a result of wars or of other causes in any part of the world'. This was a wise decision since throughout the 1950s one country after another around the world suffered the dislocation of war or natural disaster.

As a small charity, the Oxford Committee was sometimes daunted by the sheer scale of the problems it set out to relieve, but it developed its own level of expertise and began to find a niche. After the creation of Israel in 1948, the Committee provided winter clothes and supplies for needy refugees in the Middle East through the United Nations Relief and Works Agency (UNRWA).

In 1951, the value of clothes, gifts and donations reached £80,000, providing a firm base for the Committee to explore longer-term ways of helping people. Reliable partners were sought in Europe, where handcraft workshops and rehousing schemes were funded and scholarships provided; meanwhile in Jordan, the Committee made grants to hospitals and health-care programmes for Palestinian refugees.

Events in the Far East, particularly in Korea and Hong Kong, monopolized the Committee's attention in the early 1950s. By the time the Korean War ended in 1953, over three million people had died and 100,000 children were reported to be orphaned and living a hand-to-mouth existence on the streets. The Oxford Committee raised £60,000 and large amounts of clothing were dispatched to agencies like the Salvation Army working in Korea. £125,000 was also raised for Chinese refugees who had escaped to Hong Kong, where clothes and relief supplies, as well as support for small schools, vocational training, health care and community services, were paid for from donations from the British public. Today, many supporters of Oxfam Hong Kong are people who were actively helped by the Oxford Committee in the 1950s.

Howard Lesley Kirkley, appointed as General Secretary in 1951, was vital to the organization's evolution during this period. It was due mainly to Kirkley's hard work and commitment that the Oxford group transformed itself from the fledgling

Food and clothing supplies were sent to relieve suffering in post-war Europe. In Dortmund more than 160 children of the 1,737 enrolled in this feeding scheme could not attend because they had no shoes.

committee of the post-war years into the internationally respected organization of today. Prompt arrival at a disaster became Kirkley's hallmark and he put Oxfam (as it began to be known) firmly on the map as a provider of small but timely assistance for people in distress.

World Refugee Year: 1959-1960

Kirkley was invited to join the UK Committee for World Refugee Year, an opportunity that provided him with the launch pad needed to project Oxfam on to the nation's consciousness. Endorsed by the United Nations, the year aimed to raise funds to clear the remaining refugee camps in Europe and rehabilitate their inmates. The year also focused on refugees in the Middle East, Hong Kong and North Africa. The success of World Refugee Year exceeded people's expectations. By 1961, participating countries had raised a total of $91 million. Britain contributed £9 million, two-thirds of which was made up of donations from the voluntary agencies. The Oxford Committee gave a total of £775,900 and local appeal groups did much to raise awareness in towns and villages all over Britain. Coffee mornings, 'hunger lunches', concerts, school events, slide shows and other

The first Oxfam shop opened in Broad Street, Oxford in 1948 and is still in use today.

money-raising ventures were the order of the day. For the first time, the amount of cash donated by the public exceeded the value of donated goods.

Rapid growth

The surge of public interest and support generated by World Refugee Year became a massive groundswell of concern for the world's poor in the 1960s. Oxfam's annual income rose from £1 million in 1960 to £3.25 million by the end of the decade. It pioneered new ways of raising money for its ever-increasing overseas programme. By 1965, 20 regional organizers co-ordinated the activities of over 400 Oxfam groups, and Oxfam gift shops grew to number 200 by 1970, selling goods donated from the public and handcrafts from overseas. Oxfam had become a household name.

One of the ways in which Oxfam established itself as the leading charity of the decade was to introduce a hard-hitting method of fundraising, intended to shock and provoke people into action. The image of a starving child generated a huge outburst of public sympathy and concern when tragedy hit parts of the newly independent Congo in 1960. In the disruption caused by civil war, a terrible famine developed in a remote part of the country. Aware of the deteriorating situation, the Oxford Committee made an immediate grant of £5,000 to the Congolese Red Cross and followed this up with appeal letters to the press.

As well as triggering an outpouring of generosity, the image of the starving child also launched an entirely new perception of Africa in the minds of the British public. Previously seen as a continent to be explored or civilized, a land of strange customs and exotic tribes, the newly independent countries were now looked upon in a new light.

By the standards of Western affluence, their peoples were now seen as living on the very margins of existence, in a state of poverty. African countries needed substantial investment in order to 'develop'. The instrument for bringing about this development would be aid, in which donor countries would channel financial resources to the poorer nations, enabling them to build up their own social and economic institutions.

The roots of long-term development

Throughout the 1950s, Oxfam remained chiefly a food and clothing operation, providing immediate relief to hungry, sick or homeless people. Towards the end of the decade, there began the first signs of a public and political interest in longer-term development on which Oxfam decided to build.

Oxfam began to look for self-help projects to support in areas such as public health, agriculture and community development. Oxfam's response to

The 1950s were the 'Refugee Years'. Here, Palestinian families in Jordan are collecting their food rations. Oxfam still works with refugees in Jordan today, in the fields of disability and vocational training.

emergencies remained the function for which it was best known by those who were aware of the emerging organization. But those closely involved were beginning to think that prevention was better than cure, and that more resources needed to be put into helping to prevent disasters occurring in the first place.

Freedom from hunger

'If a free society cannot help the many who are poor, it can never serve the few who are rich,' said President Kennedy at the launch of the United Nation's Decade for Development, giving voice to the development crusade that politicians, opinion leaders and the public took to their hearts in the 1960s. The new crusade was greeted with enthusiasm by the voluntary agencies. Oxfam identified closely with the Freedom from Hunger Campaign (FFH) launched by the Food and Agriculture Organization (FAO) of the United Nations which aimed to combat food shortages and famine by helping people to grow enough to feed themselves without having to rely on handouts. The FAO's Director General, Dr B.J. Sen of India, asserted that the root causes of poverty needed to be addressed and that this could best be achieved by promoting self-sustaining agricultural development in poor communities to help people to break out of the poverty trap.

Endorsed by church officials and the leaders of the main political parties, the British Freedom from Hunger Campaign was launched in the Festival Hall by the Duke of Edinburgh in June 1962. Over 1,000 committees were eventually set up in towns and villages all over the country, many with the help of Oxfam's growing network of local organizers. Each group adopted an FFH-approved project around which it was able to raise awareness and money. By 1965, a total of £7 million had been donated for over 400 long-term projects.

More than any other charity in Britain, Oxfam caught the excitement and energy of the time. In 1963, in the middle of the FFH campaign, it was twenty-one years old. Many popular stars turned out for a 21st birthday party at a bread-and-water lunch in Trafalgar Square, which also launched a campaign to raise £1 million by the end of the year. The 'Hunger £ Million' achieved its target.

Above all, the 1960s were a decade for young people: many had taken the cause of world hunger to their hearts. Voluntary Service Overseas in the UK and the Peace Corps in the USA were set up to

Oxfam's 21st birthday rally in Trafalgar Square, 6 October 1963. Celebrities like Susan George and Peter Finch collected donations.

encourage young volunteers to spend time in developing countries to help people to build new skills. Politicians and opinion leaders also rose to the challenge of bringing an end to world poverty; the Overseas Development Institute was created to press for more coherent aid for underdeveloped countries; and a Ministry of Overseas Development was set up by the Labour Party in 1964, with the minister having a seat in the Cabinet.

Meanwhile, Oxfam's education and information departments were developing materials to support another important aspect of the Freedom from Hunger Campaign: the education of people, especially the younger generation, about the root causes of poverty and suffering. The materials emphasized that all people in the world depended upon each other and stressed that, given the right support, people in the Third World could make lasting improvements to their own lives. Instead of presenting a simple picture of the hungry millions, Oxfam had begun to use its own experiences of overseas development to project an alternative, and more complex, picture of the world.

Oxfam's first major step on the development path was the appointment of its first overseas field director in 1961, when Jimmy Betts was asked to set up an Oxfam office in southern Africa.

Southern Africa

Betts was to identify suitable projects and ensure that they developed. Probably the best known of the resulting work was Oxfam's programme in Bechuanaland (later Botswana), where drought had devastated farming communities. Working mainly with government departments, Betts established programmes to help farmers to improve water sources and the health of their cattle. The emphasis of much of this work was on implementing the ideas of 'aid' experts from the developed world. It was not until much later that agencies like Oxfam began to recognize that people held the key to their own development, rooted in years of experience managing their own environment. Support, tools and training were needed so that people could develop and implement their own ideas.

Partnership with indigenous agencies

Oxfam had first funded work in India in 1951, and its experience in the 1960s had a profound influence on the development of the overseas programme. Gandhi's vision of a more democratic India survived his assassination in 1948. Vinoba Bhave's *gramdan* (land-gift) movement persuaded landowners to give plots of land to the poor. Ownership of land is the most important issue for poor people. With land, a family can grow crops, raise cattle, earn a living and survive. Without land, a person is powerless, vulnerable and dependent on others.

Another follower of Gandhi was Jaya Prakesh Narayan, a politician responsible for relief efforts in Bihar in 1966, when monsoon rains failed and famine threatened the lives of over 48 million people. Oxfam's involvement in the famine relief operation brought its Field Director Jim Howard into contact with J.P. Narayan. Howard, an engineer by training, helped to start well digging and borehole drilling in Bihar to reduce people's vulnerability to droughts; and he was quickly persuaded that small-scale, village-level water schemes were the kind of long-term developments that Oxfam could usefully fund in India.

A joint rural development programme – the Oxfam Gramdan Action Programme (OGAP) – was set up in Bihar. This programme immersed Oxfam in the complexities of rural development, from which it learnt the salutary lesson that development needed to go beyond simply promoting Western ideas and technology.

Water troughs helped to prevent cattle deaths during a drought in Bechuanaland (now Botswana) in 1965.

a further £145,000 over 10 years to ensure that fresh water supplies continued to be provided.

Rural development in Tanzania

Meanwhile, in newly independent Tanzania, Julius Nyerere had set out his radical new policies of 'Ujamaa' which were hailed as the way forward by development devotees the world over. Nyerere argued that the fabric of society should be redesigned to give everyone a stake in the country's wealth and that this would uplift the poor and, in turn, create a more egalitarian and productive society. Oxfam, as a result, developed a special relationship with Tanzania in which the main funding partner was the government.

Water, or the lack of it, was a major problem in Tanzania, where 90 per cent were subsistence farmers. Over-used and dirty water sources spread severe and potentially fatal diseases, and women often had to walk miles to collect a daily supply. With this in mind, the Community Development Trust Fund (CDTF), an indigenous agency supported by the Tanzanian government, asked Oxfam to help provide villages with reliable water supplies. Oxfam responded in 1968 with a commitment of £31,000 for a village-level programme to sink 233 wells.

In keeping with the philosophy of Ujamaa, villagers provided labour to dig the wells and broke up stones for the well linings. All this was done on site using local materials which kept costs low and ensured that villagers were involved in the process and so took responsibility for their own wells. By 1971, 430 wells had been constructed and the programme was so successful that Oxfam committed

Biafra

Despite growing enthusiasm for development in the 1960s, the issue which aroused the greatest public concern was the plight of the Ibo people in eastern Nigeria. The outbreak of civil war in Nigeria in 1967 brought relief back into the headlines. The Ibo people felt unfairly treated in the Nigerian Federation and broke away to form Biafra under Colonel Ojukwu. World opinion was divided. Britain, the former colonial power, supported and armed the Federal government against the secessionists, while France quietly supported and armed Biafra.

Accusations were made that Oxfam's relief efforts in Biafra were partisan; there were also many starving and suffering people on the Federal side of the line. But opinion in Britain was overwhelmingly on the side of Biafra. After strong protests from its Field Director in Nigeria, Oxfam realized that its public statements had come close to jeopardizing its neutral stance of providing emergency assistance to both sides. A team of medical and relief staff were sent to work in an area devastated by fighting, now back in Federal hands. Oxfam thereafter continued to aid both sides, helping in a relief airlift organized by the churches, to which Oxfam of Canada made a major contribution. The conflict ended in 1970 with the defeat of Biafra. But Oxfam survived this first contact with the realities of international politics and in the eyes of most of the British public had worked hard to help those in need.

Consolidation

In the 1970s, the climate within which Oxfam operated changed significantly. The 1973 oil crisis brought about a new period of austerity in Britain and dissipated the enthusiasm shared by public and government in the 1960s for ending world hunger. The gap between rich and poor was widening. It also became evident that aid had to be dovetailed more carefully with the existing economic and cultural environment in which it was applied.

Action for world development

In this more difficult climate, Oxfam and other agencies mounted Action for World Development (AWD), a joint campaign to keep aid and long-term development in the public eye and on the government's agenda. Position papers were produced on issues such as trade and aid; a manifesto was launched; and the churches organized a National Sign-In on World Poverty when congregations signed a declaration and presented it to local MPs. Over 100 highly motivated development action groups were formed.

Nicholas Stacey, Oxfam's new Deputy Director, was optimistic that development, like Freedom from Hunger, could become an issue of mass public concern. He thought that the world's problems were too great for small voluntary agencies to solve and that large-scale investment by governments was needed to take action on behalf of the world's poor. Stacey wanted Oxfam to devote a significant proportion of its income to campaigning to make this happen. But the trustees refused; the overseas programme remained the justification for Oxfam's existence and Stacey bowed out.

Education and lobbying

While education was a permissible activity under charity law, to stray too far towards political lobbying was not. This led to an agreement between development agencies to establish an independent non-charitable body, the World Development Movement, to research and adopt campaigning positions. Oxfam and Christian Aid also launched the *New Internationalist* magazine in 1972 to promote a wider public debate on development issues, and set up Third World First, a movement to make university students more aware

of the problems and to raise funds for overseas charities.

Throughout the 1970s, Oxfam increased its public education work in the UK and Ireland, and in 1974 decided to allocate five per cent of its donated income to inform the general public about the causes of world poverty. Classroom work in schools was developed by Oxfam's education staff and a growing network of Development Education Centres was set up; Oxfam also established the Public Affairs Unit in Oxford to research and publicize particular topics in depth. In 1975, Oxfam synthesized all its ideas on development and set out its vision of the world, which remains the same today:

> Oxfam believes in the essential dignity of people and their capacity to overcome the problems and pressures which can crush or exploit them. These may be rooted in climate or geography, or in the complex areas of economics, politics and social conditions. Oxfam is a partnership of people who share this belief – people who, regardless of race, sex, religion or politics work together for the basic human rights of food, shelter and reasonable conditions of life. We believe that, if shared equitably, there are sufficient material resources in the world to enable all people to find fulfilment and to meet basic human needs. We are committed, therefore, to a process of development by peaceful means which aims to help people, especially the poor and underprivileged overseas.

A higher profile for voluntary agencies

The effects of world recession in the 1970s led to belt-tightening by governments in the developed world. Aid contributions to the Third World began to diminish. There had to be a rethink. This asserted that all governments should do more to eradicate poverty and target development aid at the poorest 40 per cent; and the UN initiated a series of international conferences on issues such as food, the environment, women, population, water and land.

The voluntary agencies contributed to this process and their participation saw a gradual raising of their profile among governments and international institutions. Working at a local level and with limited funds, the voluntary sector tended to focus its attention on small groups to ensure that its work reached specific communities in need. The larger institutions, working mainly through

Oxfam's first Director, H.L. Kirkley at the Queen Elizabeth Hospital, Umahia, during the Biafra war.

Brian Walker, reflected Oxfam's growing sensitivity towards people's needs and ideas in 1974.

The growth of Oxfam's work in Latin America coincided with a wave of new and radical views on development, expressed most strongly by the Catholic Church in the region. Priests had first-hand experience of the atrocities inflicted on poor communities. In their view, much development aid failed to improve the lives of the poor and, if it reached them at all, entrenched rather than resolved their problems.

Oxfam's main project partner in Brazil, the Federation of Organizations for Social and Educational Assistance (FASE), was influenced by the new school of thought that development was carried out by people and not for people. Run by Brazilians, FASE sought to promote community development in rural and urban areas through teams of outreach workers who offered advice about anything from agriculture to health care. Instead of measuring the success of a project by the extent to which people gained economically – with a better harvest or new health centre – FASE put more emphasis on the development process itself as a means of helping people to rebuild their self-confidence and self-respect. Influenced by thinkers such as the Brazilian educator Paolo Freire, Oxfam became convinced that the way forward had to be a process which gave people power and allowed them to learn from their experiences.

governments, could not hope to show such sensitivity to the human condition. Increased respect for the grassroots work of the voluntary agencies was demonstrated in the developing contacts between Oxfam and the Overseas Development Administration and, from the end of the 1970s, with the European Community.

Voices from overseas

'As we have gained a deeper understanding of development and a greater trust in the people we're working with, so we have tended to give more grants to local groups, getting down deeper into the grassroots where the people themselves can decide on their own priorities rather than outsiders like us imposing our ideas on them.' Oxfam's new Director,

Bangladesh

On the other side of the world, in East Pakistan (soon to become Bangladesh), similar views were being voiced by indigenous agencies. Here, too, Oxfam backed an organization – the Bangladesh Rehabilitation Assistance Committee (BRAC) – which promoted active community development.

BRAC's staff, all of them Bangladeshi, worked closely with local people to help to plan for the long term. They based their work on simple technology and affordable materials, which provided a solid platform for future activities. Fishing and agricultural co-operatives were set up which, in turn, brought in money for the community to support health, family planning, education and women's groups. By initiating a process of self-sustaining development that involved a minimum of intervention by outside agencies, BRAC ensured that the people themselves took charge and their traditional ways of life were not adversely affected by the development process. The BRAC approach soon became a model for village-level development throughout Bangladesh.

Shops – a shrewd marketing strategy

As the fund-raising climate got harsher, Oxfam had to find new ways of raising money for its ever-growing overseas programme. The philanthropic pot, already threatened by the downturn in the economy, was subject to increased competition from a growing number of charitable organizations. People began to question whether their donations would make any difference, given the size of the problems. Why try to save the world when you could see poverty on your own doorstep? Brian Walker resolved to make sure that funds continued to flow in, despite the climate of recession. Under his direction, Oxfam became more businesslike and commercially orientated, and grew substantially

Abdur Rajjak – a paramedic trained by the Bangladesh Rehabilitation Assistance Committee – at work in Derai Chandpur, Sylhet, Bangladesh, 1975.

throughout the 1970s, its income rising from just over £3 million in 1970 to just over £9.5 million in 1978-9, then to £18,756,195 in 1979-80.

In the early 1970s, nearly half of Oxfam's income was generated by its network of 250 shops run by teams of volunteers up and down the country. Brian Walker saw Oxfam shops as an opportunity to increase Oxfam's income substantially and raise its profile in the high street. Under Walker's leadership, by the end of the decade, the number of shops grew to over 500, and shop income had surpassed appeals as a source of income. The growth of the shop network coincided with an increased professionalism; shops on permanent high-street sites gradually replaced smaller rent-free concerns and shop helpers were given training in pricing, publicity and display.

Oxfam Trading

Oxfam's serious entry into retailing coincided with a decision to transform Oxfam Trading's existing Christmas card and basic product line into a thriving mail order business. By 1975, Oxfam

Trading's profits had risen to £750,000, chiefly due to a Helping by Selling scheme which marketed handcrafts produced by small-scale enterprises in developing countries. Unlike other organizations, Oxfam Trading's new Bridge scheme existed primarily to serve the producer groups, in the same way that Oxfam funded projects overseas. To reduce the producer's dependency on the whims of the British market, Bridge offered fair prices for the handcrafts and ensured that 40 per cent of the order was paid in advance. Most importantly, the scheme also reinvested any profits, either as dividends for the producer groups themselves, or in a development fund which provided technical advice, training and equipment for new initiatives. By the early 1980s, Oxfam Trading's sales had risen to over £1 million annually and field officers had been recruited in India and Bangladesh, and later in Thailand, Indonesia and Mexico.

Oxfam goes green

As people were becoming disenchanted with the philosophy of the throwaway society, Guy Stringer, Oxfam's new Deputy Director, developed an original idea of Lesley Kirkley's for a recycling plant which would both benefit the environment and raise funds for Oxfam's work. After a detailed study of the financial viability of recycling, the Wastesaver Centre was established in a derelict textile mill in Huddersfield (1975) to recycle anything from bottle tops to old clothes. The bulk of the sacks, containing aluminium and rags, were dispatched from Oxfam shops up and down the country. At its height, 60 staff and 60 young people on job creation schemes processed tin, paper, plastics, furniture, textiles and aluminium, all of which were reused by industry. But, by 1979, the bottom had fallen out of the waste products market and Wastesaver was forced to

Manapad women workers at the Palm Leaf Cooperative in South India supplied Oxfam Trading with their products for many years through the 'Brigade' programme.

Good quality 'Bridge' craft products on display in an Oxfam shop.

streamline its operation. A move to smaller premises, where fewer staff processed a smaller selection of materials, enabled Wastesaver to carry on and to continue to generate funds for Oxfam out of textiles and aluminium.

Disasters, recovery and Cambodia

Despite its evolution into a development agency, Oxfam continued to provide emergency assistance at times of crisis and, where possible, tried to promote long-term recovery in the wake of disasters. When vast numbers of people sought refuge in India during the Bangladesh war of independence in 1972, Oxfam adopted the policy of hiring relief helpers and purchasing supplies locally, which was both more effective and more economic. In northern Ethiopia in 1973, where a hidden famine cost many thousands of lives, Oxfam allocated £192,233 for relief supplies; and in Western India, when drought hit Maharashtra State, Oxfam worked with local people to set up a network of feeding centres. In 1976, after an earthquake in Guatemala, Oxfam was quick to respond, providing corrugated iron sheeting for shelter, and making emergency grants totalling over £1 million for the first time ever; and, when thousands of Vietnamese boat people arrived in Hong Kong in 1979, Oxfam provided sanitation and water supplies for refugees.

After the Vietnamese invasion brought an end to Pol Pot's brutal regime in Kampuchea in 1979, the huge scale of the four-year tragedy began to unfold. Journalists and aid workers, allowed into what had been a closed country, witnessed the mass graves and horrors of the killing fields and reported the deaths of well over a million people. Almost all skilled professional people had been killed by the Khmer Rouge, while thousands of others had died from overwork, disease or starvation. Education and health services were virtually non-existent; industry, transport and agriculture in ruins; land and villages lay abandoned and towns were empty.

The plight of the Kampuchean people occupied many of Oxfam's staff and volunteers for much of the time in 1979. Realizing that huge sums of money would be needed for the relief effort, and given that the United Nations did not recognize the new Vietnamese-backed government as legitimate, Brian Walker took the decision to intervene in Kampuchea directly. Oxfam and other non-governmental agencies formed a Consortium

which agreed to channel donations and supplies through Oxfam. A massive relief effort had begun from which Oxfam was to emerge with a new prominence and prestige, and with a greatly enhanced reputation.

Oxfam was inundated with donations amounting to £500,000. *Blue Peter*'s bring and buy appeal for Oxfam, the first time a television appeal had been linked to a named charity, evoked an even greater response. The grand total of £3.5 million exceeded all expectations.

Based in Phnom Penh, the Consortium members played an important role in humanitarian relief. The most dramatic contribution by Oxfam was to open up the sea route from Singapore, bringing in a barge 'the size of a football pitch' loaded with supplies. These achievements, and later the provision of seed, trucks and medical supplies on a large scale, were warmly welcomed by the Kampuchean authorities, and excited the admiration of the world.

Supplies of rice, seeds, hoes, water pumps and fertilizers were sent to rural areas; and equipment and materials arrived in Phnom Penh to rebuild the city water works. In its first year, the Consortium spent £12 million, over half of which was contributed by Oxfam in the largest voluntary relief operation to date.

In 1983, with the emergency officially over, Oxfam continued its support for the country which desperately needed substantial long-term investment to rebuild after the crisis. Over the next 10 years, Oxfam and a handful of other agencies tried to provide the people of what was called Cambodia again with equipment and training to help to rebuild its shattered economy. But a long-term solution to Cambodia's problems depended on major international economic aid and investment, and an acceptable and lasting internal settlement.

A new role for Oxfam (1980-92)

'Five million pounds for some thirty emergencies was a tragic all-time record,' reported Oxfam's Annual Review for 1983-4. Torrential rains had caused flooding in Ecuador; Peru was hit by a devastating drought; severe floods in South India displaced thousands of people; and in Vietnam livelihoods were shattered by typhoons. Drought also affected large parts of Africa, from the Sahel to the Horn, and a wide belt in the south. Oxfam responded in all cases – providing emergency relief, rehabilitation assistance and by sending in experienced staff to offer training and support where necessary.

To these 'natural' disasters were added the appalling consequences of man-made crises: the refugees and people displaced by civil war, riots, 'security operations' and insurgency. In 1989, the United Nations Disarmament Committee reported that out of 127 wars fought since World War II, 125 have been in developing countries, accounting for upwards of 21 million deaths.

In El Salvador and Guatemala, as years of development work were destroyed, and friends and colleagues were harassed and even killed by paramilitary forces, Oxfam channelled funds to support displaced people and refugees who had escaped across borders to safety. In Nicaragua, where thousands of people were re-settled away from border fighting, Oxfam paid for temporary housing and medical kits for health workers. Funds for clean water supplies and sanitation facilities were provided to local groups in south Lebanon, where ten years of war had caused great suffering, and in Sri Lanka, a country torn apart by civil strife, Oxfam made grants to local organizations for humanitarian relief.

The people who suffer most from violent conflict are civilians, and the targeting of innocent people is now a deliberate weapon of war. Women are particularly hard-hit, as most of the active men are either involved in the fighting or are forced to migrate in search of work because of the disruption that war causes to agriculture and the traditional economy. Conflict impedes development: land is abandoned or destroyed; livelihoods can no longer be sustained; and people become poorer and, as a consequence, more vulnerable to disasters. It is not surprising therefore that much of Oxfam's work takes place in parts of the world where people have suffered the dislocation of war.

Deepening crisis in Africa

At the beginning of the 1980s, Oxfam became increasingly concerned about reports of suffering in the Horn of Africa, caused by the combined effects of political unrest, fighting and drought. A joint agency appeal, launched by the Disasters Emergency Committee in June 1980, raised £2 million for relief work in Ethiopia, Sudan, Kenya, Somalia and Uganda. In some countries, where the spectre of famine began to recede, Oxfam was able to channel support into rehabilitation programmes. In Uganda, for instance, Oxfam supplied seed from areas not affected by the drought to people in the famine areas so that they could start farming again and rediscover self-sufficiency. But, in the case of Ethiopia, the years of drought and fighting had caused such misery and dislocation that as many as 3.5 million people still remained short of food.

Three natural disasters led to the major tragedy of the Horn of Africa. In 1980, the rains were only a third of normal as the area was recovering from the famine of the mid-1970s. Serious locust attacks in the early 1980s made things worse. Grain reserves in the region were very low. Soon cattle began to die and families had to leave their homes in search of food and water. The war between the central government in Addis Ababa and the northern provinces of Tigray and Eritrea further added to the problem as resources were diverted into arms instead of food. By 1984, when the rains failed again, the situation grew desperate. In the Ethiopian provinces of Gondar and Wollo, up to eight million people were suffering from severe malnutrition and, cut off from emergency supplies, the people of Tigray and Eritrea were exposed to the double tragedy of drought and war. In Tigray alone, hundreds of thousands of people died and a further two million people were threatened with starvation.

Despite warnings from the Ethiopian government that it would not take much to tip the balance into crisis, the international support needed to avert the devastating famine of 1984-5 was not forthcoming. Oxfam and other agencies did what they could to raise funds for emergency relief, and to heighten the world's awareness of the tragedy, but it took Michael Buerk's unforgettable reports on BBC television to awaken the world to the massive scale of the catastrophe. From this point onwards, money began to pour in to Oxfam and other agencies working in the Horn. While the people of Britain dug deep into their pockets in response to the scale of human suffering, the rock musician Bob Geldof organized an event that would capture the imagination of millions of people. The Live Aid concert galvanized people all over the globe.

In 1984–5 Oxfam allocated £21.7 million for emergency relief in the Horn of Africa, thanks to a massive increase in its income, which rose from £23 million in 1983–4 to £51 million in 1984–5. Oxfam's Famine Recovery Fund launched on television by Glenda Jackson helped to generate funds for rehabilitation work, and Comic Relief's emphasis on the human aspects of rebuilding after the crisis also boosted Oxfam's income.

Phnom Penh in 1979 after the end of Pol Pot's regime.

Hungry for change

The generous public response to famine appeals by Oxfam and other agencies was matched by concern and determination to call for changes in those policies and practices that allowed people to remain in abject poverty in the Third World. The Brandt Report of 1982 re-awakened high-level debate about relationships between rich and poor nations, but the message of Brandt did not have much public support until the Ethiopian famine occurred.

In 1984, the launch of a major new campaign – Hungry for Change (HFC) – attracted considerable media attention, and by the following year over 150 HFC groups had been set up in the UK and Ireland. Many thousands of new supporters joined with other aid agencies in a mass lobby of Parliament on the anniversary of Michael Buerk's coverage of Ethiopia. Their presence drew attention to a number of international issues which crucially affected people in the Third World. The debt crisis, reductions in government aid, worsening trade terms, the high level of arms sales and growing environmental degradation, all contributed to a world which trapped poor people in the downward spiral of poverty.

Throughout the 1980s, Oxfam continued to address international issues and to campaign for a better deal for the world's poor. In 1988, after a visit to war-torn Mozambique where thousands of people had been killed or displaced by the civil war, Oxfam's Director, Frank Judd, reported: 'Witnessing such horrors, how can we remain silent about those who support this evil? How can we fail to ask what can and should be done to stop the wickedness? To settle for treating the symptoms alone would frequently betray the poor. We must do still more to persuade our nation as a whole to match our own resolve. Neither in the UK or Ireland can we become a substitute for national commitment.'

At the end of the 1980s, Oxfam launched two major campaigns: Free Front Line Africa and a second Cambodia campaign. Both were pressed forcefully and both tested the limits of charity law, resulting in a warning from the Charity Commission that Oxfam, as a charity, should not stray into the realms of political advocacy.

The main focus of activity for Free Front Line Africa was a Front Line Fortnight in 1990 which raised public awareness of some of the obstacles to development in southern Africa. The campaign culminated in a high-profile presentation of 65,000 signed declarations to Linda Chalker, Minister of State for Overseas Development, in December 1990 and raised over £1 million for Oxfam's work in the region.

The second campaign for Cambodia was launched in 1988, amid growing fears that the Khmer Rouge, having rebuilt their forces in exile on the Thai border, were planning a return to power. A television documentary featuring Julie Christie achieved widespread media coverage; *Blue Peter* made Cambodia the subject of its 1988 Appeal; the Cambodian National Dance company, whose skills had all but been destroyed under Pol Pot, toured Britain to heighten awareness of Cambodia and its culture; and John Pilger's documentary, *Cambodia: The Betrayal*, generated the same upsurge of public concern as *Year Zero* had done ten years before, again raising Oxfam's profile.

Into the 1990s

As Oxfam approaches its 50th Anniversary, the sad fact is that, for many people around the world, things are not getting better; they are getting worse.

As the twentieth century draws to a close, more than a billion people still live in abject poverty. One in three of the world's population does not have enough to eat, and the rich countries of the North, with only 25 per cent of the world's people, consume 80 per cent of the world's resources.

The debt crisis has inflicted terrible suffering on millions of people in the developing world. In 1989, developing countries paid $52 billion more to the rich world in debt repayments and interest than they received in aid and new loans! Third World countries had to tighten their belts just to meet the

interest payments on existing loans. The people who suffer most as a result are the poor, as the first cutbacks are the health, education and social services which are so vital to improving people's lives and to instigating sustainable development.

To pay off their national debts, developing countries have been encouraged to increase their exports to earn hard currency. But, at the same time, the money they receive for these exports has been steadily reduced. The only response is to export more. As a result, the world market is saturated with primary commodities and cash crops all chasing the same markets. The value of bananas today is 33 per cent lower than it was in 1965 and banana-growing countries now have to grow six times as many crops to earn the same amount as they did in the mid-1960s.

The effect of these policies on the Third World has been catastrophic and many countries have exploited their natural resources on a massive scale. Hardwood forests are being devastated, the oceans overfished, and the land changed beyond all recognition to make way for dams, mines and other large-scale developments. Traditional patterns of life are rapidly disappearing.

Worsening trade terms and growing debt have made developing countries increasingly vulnerable in the 1990s and, to make matters worse, international development aid has also declined in real terms. On average, the richest nations now

A feeding centre at Ajeba Borara during the Ethiopian famine of 1984.

Celebrities and politicians helped to launch Oxfam's Hungry for Change campaign in October 1984.

allocate 0.36 per cent of their gross national product to overseas development, which falls far short of the United Nations' recommendation of 0.7 per cent. Of a total of $51 billion earmarked in 1988 for development aid, 48 per cent was directed at high- and middle-income countries, and much went to support large-scale programmes that did little to target the poor.

Increasing poverty is a major reason why the number of disasters has increased with every decade: from 523 in the 1960s, to 767 in the 1970s, to 1,387 in the 1980s. In 1991 alone, a series of harrowing disasters dominated our television screens: the Kurdish refugees; famine in Ethiopia, Sudan, Mozambique and Liberia; floods in Bangladesh; cholera in Peru and Africa. Only an urgent and concerted effort by the international community to tackle the causes of poverty will prevent the figure continuing to rise year by year.

It's time for a fairer world

Oxfam entered its fiftieth year in October 1991. To mark this event, and to draw attention to the continuing plight of so many people in the developing world, Oxfam launched a new campaign: It's Time for a Fairer World. At its launch, Oxfam's new Director, David Bryer, said: 'The sheer scale of poverty in developing countries is not only immoral but unnecessary and avoidable. It is our belief that if action is not taken now, the effects of that poverty pose a threat to the future of all of us in the North and South alike.'

As well as warning of the long-term global implications of failing to tackle world poverty, the campaign also reflects the unique opportunity that the world now has to move forwards. The 1990s have already seen a period of unprecedented change. The reverberations from the fall of the Berlin Wall continue to echo around the world. A new sense of international collaboration between nations is in the air, although the 'shock of the new' following the changes in Eastern Europe and the former USSR still proves disorientating for many.

It was popular pressure that triggered the changes throughout Eastern Europe and the former Soviet Union. In other parts of the world, ordinary people are also demanding democracy and greater participation in deciding their own futures. Seemingly insoluble conflicts in Angola, Ethiopia and Cambodia are being resolved, and South Africa is moving towards a new future. The United Nations faces a new dynamic role of resolving conflict and in creating a more democratic international order.

The problems of debt and terms of trade, of unnecessary arms sales, of environmental degradation will not go away, but they are all capable of solution if the world community has the will. It is Oxfam's hope, and surely the hope of all readers of this book, that the international community will seize this opportunity and rise to the challenge of tackling world poverty.

Photographers

Bangladesh	Shahildul Alam
Chile	Julio Etchart
Dominican Republic	Philip Wolmuth
Ecuador	Julio Etchart
India	Rajendra Shaw
Israel	John Tordai
Philippines	Nancy Durrell-McKenna
Senegal	Jeremy Hartley
Uganda	Jenny Mathews
Vietnam	Keith Bernstein

Text: Lucy Mitchell, Oxfam Writers Unit
Photography co-ordination: Liz Clayton, Oxfam Audio Visual Resources Unit
Project co-ordination: Robert Cornford, Oxfam Anniversary Publications

An exhibition of photographs associated with *Oxfam 50* opened at MOMA (Museum of Modern Art) in Oxford in November 1992 and will tour exhibition venues and galleries. For information about this exhibition contact Liz Clayton, OXFAM AVRU, 274 Banbury Road, Oxford OX2 7DZ.

About Oxfam
Oxfam is an international family of independent agencies. For more information about Oxfam's work, contact your local office.
in England: OXFAM, Anniversary Information, 274 Banbury Road, Oxford OX2 7DZ
in Ireland: OXFAM, 202 Lower Rathmines Road, Dublin 6
in Northern Ireland: OXFAM, PO Box 70, 52-54 Dublin Road, Belfast BT2 7HN
in Scotland: OXFAM, Fleming House, 5th Floor, 134 Renfrew Street, Glasgow G3 3T
in Wales: OXFAM, 46-48 Station Road, Llanishen, Cardiff CF4 5LU
in Australia: Community Aid Abroad, 156 George Street, Fitzroy, Victoria 3065
in Belgium: OXFAM Belgique, 39 Rue du Conseil, 1050 Bruxelles
in Canada: OXFAM Canada, 251 Laurier Avenue West, Room 301, Ottawa, Ontario K1P 5J6
in Hong Kong: OXFAM, Ground Floor - 3B, June Garden, 28 Tung Chau Street, Tai Kok Tsui, Kowloon, Hong Kong
in New Zealand: OXFAM New Zealand, Room 101 La Gonda House, 203 Karangahape Road, Auckland 1
in Quebec: OXFAM Quebec, 169 Rue St. Paul est, Montreal 127, Quebec H2Y 1G8
in the USA: OXFAM America, 115 Broadway, Boston, Massachusetts 02116